ENTRELAC PATTERN:

First Color Strip: (This strip begins and ends with a triangle). With COL A, ch required amount loosely. **Beginning triangle;**

Row 1, draw up a loop in 2nd ch from hook (2 loops on hook) YO draw thru both loops.

Row 2, insert hook between first 2 vertical bars and pick up a loop, then pick up a loop from the chain (3 loops on hook), work off by YO, draw thru 2 loops, twice, 1 loop left on hook.

Row 3, insert hook BETWEEN first 2 bars (inc made) and pick up a loop, draw up a loop from under next bar and the next ch (4 loops on hook), {YO draw thru 2 loops} 3 times (1 loop left on hook). Continue in this manner, having 1 st more each row, till you have 7 loops on hook, work them off as before, then bind off as follows: insert hook under next bar, draw yarn through bar and loop on hook (slip st worked) continue to work slip st through each bar to end.

 Slip st in SAME ch as last loop of row 5. DO NOT END OFF continue making next square as follows:

SQUARE ONE: (we are still on color strip one) Draw up a loop in each of the next 6 chains (7 loops on hook) {YO and draw through 2 loops} 6 times (1 loop left on hook) This loop is the first loop of the following row.

Row 2, insert hook under the next bar, draw yarn through (2 loops on hook) draw up loop in each of next 4 bars, draw up a loop in next ch (7 loops on hook), work off loops as row 1 of square.

Rows 3-5 rep row 2, bind off this square by slip st in each bar to end, slip st same ch as last loop of row 5.

SQUARE TWO: (we are still on color strip one) Draw up a loop in each of the next 6 ch (7 loops on hook), work off as before, complete same as square 1. Con't in this way until there are 6 chains left at end of row.

ENDING TRIANGLE (we are now at the end of the first color strip) Draw up 6 loops in rem chains in addition to the one on hook, work off as before, next row draw up 5 loops, plus 1 on hook, work off as before, Con't in this manner, always having 1 less loop each row, until 1 rem, end off. This completes the first color strip.

SECOND COLOR STRIP: This color strip begins and ends with a square. Each square has 5 rows.

SQUARE 1. With Col B, pick up 1 loop in each of 6 slip sts of the beginning triangle, pick up a loop in end of first row of first square on strip 1 (7 loops on hook), work off loops as before. Con't in this manner as in square l, picking up the first set of sts in the slipped sts, then under the bars in subsequent rows, you will always have one loop on hook picking up 5 more loops, and the 7th st will be picked up in the end rows of the first square on strip 1(along the side edge), instead of the chains.

When 5 rows are completed, slip st under each bar, having last slip st in the last row (top point) of the same square. Con't in this manner, always picking up 5 loops (one already on hook makes 6 loops on hook) and the 7th st in end of rows on next square. Continue across row, ending with a completed square

THIRD COLOR STRIP: With COL C, Begins and ends with a triangle. Begin triangle as follows: With MC ch 2, draw up a loop in the first ch from hook and pick up a loop in side of first row of first square of color strip 2 (3 loops on hook) {YO and draw thru 2 loops} twice. Rep from * to * of first strip triangle 1, slip st in first bound off st of square 1 strip 2. Work squares across row, ending with a triangle as ending triangle color strip 1.

Tunisian Cables to Crochet™

Tunisian Cables to Crochet
Introduction

True Tunisian cables are made to look like handknit cables.

Cables are made in the same fashion as other stitches. The only difference is that, at the cabling point, you cross the stitches to work them out of order. It's a very easy process.

Learn the cabling technique with 11 projects. Some projects are designed so that a regular crochet hook can be used instead of a Tunisian afghan hook. A crochet hook without a thumb rest is recommended. Although a thumb rest doesn't necessarily cause a physical problem with working the stitches, it can be difficult at times to slip the stitches over the thumb rest without a struggle.

The cables are made on the return pass, or the closing pass. You will simply remove the required number of loops from the hook, cross them and place them back on the hook before completing the closing.

The major difference in the closing is an extra chain in the center of the cables. The chain is included in subsequent rows as well. The extra chain, however, is ignored when working the subsequent rows. It is worked solely to allow the cable to open up rather than sit flat.

As with all my current patterns, there is a "chain 1" at the beginning of all closing rows. Traditionally, "yarn over, pull through 1 loop on hook" has been used. However, due to the evolution of Tunisian crochet in recent years, this instruction has been changed to "chain 1." Since some patterns will include more than 1 chain at the beginning of the closing, it is essential that there is specificity as to which chain to use in the subsequent row.

Both left- and right-handed crocheters can enjoy Tunisian crochet. Although instructions aren't right-hand specific, the application of a cable is directionally specific. A right-leaning cable is labled as "right" leaning. A left-handed crocheter, following the instructions exactly, will have a mirror image and their cable will be left-leaning. A left-hander can either follow instructions and end with a mirror image, which won't matter in most patterns or he or she will need to switch instructions for right-leaning and left-leaning if an exact duplicate is desired.

This mirror-image effect is also evident in the instructions for a directionally specific right- or left-leaning decrease. The "leans" will be in the opposite direction for a left-handed crocheter. But it will not affect the finished project. ∎

Contents

Basic Stitches

GETTING STARTED: These are all side-to-side insertions. They can be worked by both right- and left-handed crocheters.

TYPICAL FOUNDATION: Chain number as stated in instructions, working in **back bar of chain** (*see illustration*) and holding back all lps on hook, insert hook in 2nd ch from hook, yo, pull lp through, [insert hook in next ch, yo, pull lp through] in each ch across. You will have the same amount of lps on hook as number chained.

Back Bar of Chain

TUNISIAN SIMPLE STITCH (TSS): Insert hook under front vertical bar from side-to-side (*right to left for right-handers or left to right for left-handers*) (*see Photo A*), yo, pull lp through (*see Photo B*).

PHOTO A

PHOTO B

TUNISIAN KNIT STITCH (TKS): Insert hook from front to back (*see Photo A*) between front and back vertical bars (*see Photo B*) of same st, yo, pull lp through (*see Photo C*).

PHOTO A

PHOTO B

PHOTO C

TUNISIAN TWISTED PURL STITCH (TTPS): With yarn in front, insert hook from front of work to back under back vertical bar *(see Photo A)*, pulling back vertical bar toward front of work, yo *(see Photo B)*, pull lp through. The stitch is wrapped with front yarn.

PHOTO A

TUNISIAN PURL STITCH (TPS): Bring yarn to front of work *(see Photo A)*; insert hook under next front vertical bar, yo, pull lp through *(see Photo B)*. The stitch is wrapped with front yarn.

PHOTO A

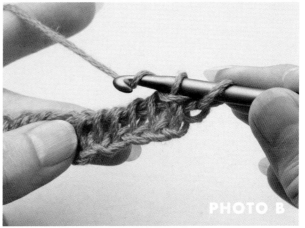

PHOTO B

PHOTO B

TUNISIAN EXTENDED STITCH (TES): Insert hook from front to back *(see Photo A)* between front and back vertical bars *(see Photo B)* of same st *(as for TKS)*, yo, pull lp through *(see Photo C)*, ch 1.

PHOTO A

PHOTO B

PHOTO C

FINISHING

For the projects in this book, a particular type of seaming is preferred. To begin seaming in Mattress Stitch, thread a yarn needle with the same yarn used in the project. Hold the two edges parallel with right sides of the fabric facing you and beginning edge at the bottom. If desired, loosely pin the edges together. Insert the needle from side-to-side under the 2 outermost front vertical bars of the first side edge, pull the yarn through, leaving a 5-inch tail. Insert the needle from side-to-side under the 2 outermost front vertical bars of the second side edge.

Still on the second side edge, insert the needle from side-to-side in the next row up under the 2 outermost front vertical bars. Now, returning to the first side edge, insert the needle from side-to-side under the same bars as the original insertion. Still on the first side edge, move up one row, and insert the needle under the 2 outermost front vertical bars of that row. Once again, returning to the second side edge, insert the needle from side-to-side under the same bars as the previous insertion.

Continue working back and forth on the two pieces in the same manner for about an inch, then gently pull on the yarn to snug the two pieces together. Continue until seam is complete, pulling seam closed every inch or so. Weave in the tail. Use the beginning tail to even-up the lower edge by working a figure 8 between the stitches at the corners. Insert the threaded needle from front to back under both threads of the corner stitch on the edge opposite the tail, then into the same stitch on the first edge. Pull gently until the "8" fills the gap. When a project is made with a textured yarn that will not pull easily through the pieces, use a smooth yarn of the same color to work the seam. ■

Step-by-Step
Tunisian Crochet Cables

For the projects in this book, all the cables are made during the closing *(or return)* pass. This is the 2nd half of each row *(B)*. The first half of the row is worked normally *(A)*.

When closing the stitches, once you reach the point of the cable, you will simply rearrange the cable stitches on the hook.

The cables in this book are all split down the center. When there are 6-stitch cables, the cables are crossed, 3 over or under 3. For 4-stitch cables, the cables are crossed 2 over or under 2.

All cables are written so that you will not need a cable stitch holder, but you will need an extra crochet hook.

STARTING THE CABLE

Remove the working loop from the hook and gently lengthen it slightly. Remove the indicated number of stitches from the hook. For a 4-stitch cable, remove 4 loops *(see Photo A)*. For a 6-stitch cable, remove 6 loops *(see Photo B)*.

PHOTO B

For the remaining photos, a 6-stitch cable is shown. The same procedure is used for any number of cable stitches.

RIGHT-LEANING CABLE (RLC)

Pinch the last half of the cable stitches to the back of work *(see photo C)* with the non-hook hand and replace the first half of the cable stitches on the Tunisian crochet hook.

PHOTO A

PHOTO C

Working from back, with regular crochet hook (*see photo D*), replace the remaining loops onto the Tunisian crochet hook.

PHOTO D

The stitches are now redistributed, out of order.

Replace working lp (*see photo E*) that you removed at the beginning of your cable and tighten as necessary.

PHOTO E

There is one more step to complete the cable. Closing the stitches is explained in the next section. This instruction is considered part of the cable and is not included in the pattern instruction.

CLOSING THE STITCHES

For a 6-stitch cable: [Yarn over, pull through 2 loops on hook] 3 times, chain 1, [yarn over, pull through 2 loops on hook] 3 times. 6-stitch cable complete.

For a 4-stitch cable: [Yarn over, pull through 2 loops on hook] twice, chain 1, [yarn over, pull through 2 loops on hook] twice. 4-stitch cable complete.

LEFT-LEANING CABLE (LLC)

Pinch the last half of the cable stitches to the front of work with (*see photo F*) the non-hook hand and replace the first half of the cable stitches on the Tunisian crochet hook.

PHOTO F

Working from front, with regular crochet hook (*see photo G*), replace the remaining loops onto the Tunisian crochet hook.

PHOTO G

The stitches are now redistributed *(see photo H),* out of order.

PHOTO H

There is one more step to complete the cable. Closing the stitches is explained in the next section. This instruction is considered part of the cable and is not included in the pattern instruction.

CLOSING THE STITCHES

For a 6-stitch cable: [Yarn over, pull through 2 loops on hook] 3 times, chain 1, [yarn over, pull through 2 loops on hook] 3 times. 6-stitch cable complete.

For a 4-stitch cable: [Yarn over, pull through 2 loops on hook] twice, chain 1, [yarn over, pull through 2 loops on hook] twice. 4-stitch cable complete.

CONTINUING

Like most cables in any type of needlework, the first crossing of the stitches will look more like a jumble of stitches rather than a nice cable. It is only upon working the subsequent rows that the cable will start forming.

When working the row directly after the cable crossing, pull up on the chain 1 *(see photo I)* in the center of the cable with your non-hook hand to extend the stitches and be able to work into them easier. ∎

PHOTO I

SKILL LEVEL

INTERMEDIATE

FINISHED SIZES
Scarf (blocked): 5 x 52 inches

Headband (blocked): 2 x 19 inches; stretches to fit up to 24-inch circumference

MATERIALS
- Red Heart Stardust superfine (fingering) weight yarn (1¾ oz/191 yds/50g per skein):
    3 skeins #1303 brown
- Size H/8/5mm Tunisian crochet hook, minimum lengths of 6 and 24 inches, or size needed to obtain gauge
- Size G/6/4mm crochet hook
- Tapestry needle

GAUGE
Size H hook: 10-st cable section 1¼ x 3 inches; 15 rows = 3 inches blocked

PATTERN NOTES
When minimum length of hook needed is 6 inches, a regular crochet hook, without thumb rest, can be used.

Project made by making first Cable Stitch Strip. Drop stitches are created along the sides of rows of first Strip. Next, Cable Stitch Strip is made in join-as-you-go method, then subsequent drop-stitch row and final Cable Stitch Strip is worked at end.

See Introduction for information on "mirror image" for left-handed crocheters.

Last loop on hook is counted as first loop of next row unless otherwise stated.

Join with slip stitch as indicated unless otherwise stated.

These projects use Right-Leaning 6-stitch cables (RLC). See pages 7 and 8 for detailed instructions.

SCARF
FIRST CABLE STRIP
Row 1:

 A. With 6-inch size H hook, ch 10, work **typical foundation** *(see page 4) (10 lps on hook)*;

 B. ch 1, [yo, pull through 2 lps on hook] across, leaving **last lp on hook** *(see Pattern Notes)*.

Row 2:

 A. Sk first vertical bar, **TTPS** *(see page 5)*, **TKS** *(see page 4)* across to last 2 sts, TTPS, TKS *(10 lps on hook)*;

 B. ch 1, [yo, pull through 2 lps on hook] across.

GENEVA
Scarf & Headband

Rows 3 & 4: Rep row 2.

Row 5:

  A. Sk first vertical bar, TTPS, TKS across to last 2 sts, TTPS, TKS *(10 lps on hook)*;

  B. ch 1, yo, pull lp though 2 lps on hook, **RLC** *(see page 7)*, [yo, pull through 2 lps on hook] twice.

Row 6: When creating all following rows, ignore ch-1 sp in center of each cable:

  A. Sk first vertical bar, TTPS, TKS across to last 2 sts, TTPS, TKS *(10 lps on hook)*;

  B. ch 1, [yo, pull lp through 2 lps on hook] 4 times, ch 1, [yo, pull through 2 lps on hook] 5 times.

Rows 7–9: Rep row 6.

Rows 10–259: [Rep rows 5–9 consecutively] 50 times.

Row 260: Rep row 5.

Row 261:

  A. Sk first vertical bar, TTPS, TKS across to last 2 sts, TTPS, TKS *(10 lps on hook)*;

  B. ch 1, [yo, pull through 2 lps on hook] across.

Last row: Sk first vertical bar, insert hook in next st as for TTPS, yo, pull lp through st and through lp on hook *(sl st made)*, sl st as for TKS across to last 2 sts, sl st as for TTPS in next st, sl st as for TKS in last st. Fasten off.

DROP STITCH INSERT

Getting Started: Turn Cable Strip to begin work along side in ends of rows. Only 1 row is completed.

When dropping the yarn over in part B, allow it to drop off completely and it will not be worked. Its purpose is to create the height of the drop stitch.

A. With 24-inch size H hook, **join** (*see Pattern Notes*) in end of first row, ch 1, insert hook in end of next row, yo, pull lp through, [yo, insert hook in end of next row, yo, pull lp through] across to last row, yo, insert hook in end of last row, yo, pull lp through (*520 lps on hook*);

B. ch 1, [remove working lp from hook and next yo, allowing yo to drop off hook completely, replace working lp on hook, yo, pull through 2 lps on hook] across to last 3 lps rem on hook, [yo, pull through 2 lps on hook] twice.

2ND CABLE STRIP
Row 1:

A. With 6-inch size H hook, ch 10, work typical foundation across to last ch, insert hook in last ch and in top of first st of Drop Stitch Insert as for TKS, yo, pull through both sts at same time (*10 lps on hook*);

B. there is no ch-1 at the beg of joining row, [yo, pull through 2 lps on hook] across.

Row 2:

A. Sk first vertical bar, TTPS, TKS across to last 2 sts, TTPS, insert hook in last st as for **TSS** (*see page 4*) and in next st of Drop Stitch Insert as for TKS, yo, pull lp through both sts at same time (*10 lps on hook*);

B. [yo, pull through 2 lps on hook] across.

Rows 3 & 4: Rep row 2.

Row 5:

A. Sk first vertical bar, TTPS, TKS across to last 2 sts, TTPS, insert hook in last st as for TSS and in next st of Drop Stitch Insert as for TKS, yo, pull lp through both sts at same time (*10 lps on hook*);

B. yo, pull lp through 2 lps on hook, RLC, [yo, pull through 2 lps on hook] twice.

Row 6: When creating all following rows, ignore the ch-1 sp in the middle of each cable:

A. Sk first vertical bar, TTPS, TKS across to last 2 sts, TTPS, insert hook in last st as for TSS and in next st of Drop Stitch Insert as for TKS, yo, pull through both sts at same time (*10 lps on hook*);

B. [yo, pull lp through 2 lps on hook] 4 times, ch 1, [yo, pull through 2 lps on hook] 5 times.

Rows 7–9: Rep row 6.

Rows 10–259: [Rep rows 5–9 consecutively] 50 times.

Row 260: Rep row 5.

Row 261:

A. Sk first vertical bar, TTPS, TKS across to last 2 sts, TTPS, insert hook in last st as for TSS and in next st of Drop Stitch Insert as for TKS, yo, pull lp through both sts at same time (*10 lps on hook*);

B. [yo, pull through 2 lps on hook] across.

Last row: Sk first vertical bar, insert hook in next st as for TTPS, yo, pull lp through st and through lp on hook (*sl st made*), sl st as for TKS across to last 2 sts, sl st as for TTPS in next st, insert hook in last st as for TSS and in final row of Drop Stitch Insert as for TKS, yo, pull lp through both sts at same time and through lp on hook. Fasten off.

DROP STITCH INSERT
Rep Drop Stitch Insert along side in ends of rows of 2nd Cable Strip.

3RD CABLE STRIP
Work 3rd Cable Strip as for 2nd Cable Strip.

FINISHING
If desired, completely immerse project in cool water, squeeze lightly, roll in clean towel to remove excess water, lie flat, shape and allow to air dry.

HEADBAND
Getting Started: Project made by making Cable Strip, then seaming first row to last row to form a ring.

Row 1:

A. With 6-inch size H hook, ch 16, work **typical foundation** (*see page 4*) (*16 lps on hook*);

B. ch 1, [yo, pull through 2 lps on hook] across, leaving **last lp on hook** (*see Pattern Notes*).

Row 2:

A. Sk first vertical bar, **TTPS** (*see page 5*), **TKS** (*see page 4*) across to last 2 sts, TTPS, TKS (*16 lps on hook*);

B. ch 1, [yo, pull through 2 lps on hook] across.

Rows 3 & 4: Rep row 2.

Row 5:

A. Sk first vertical bar, TTPS, TKS across to last 2 sts, TTPS, TKS (*16 lps on hook*);

B. ch 1, yo, pull through 2 lps on hook, **RLC** (*see page 7*) twice, [yo, pull through 2 lps on hook] twice.

Row 6: When creating all following rows, ignore the ch-1 sp in the center of each cable:

A. Sk first vertical bar, TTPS, TKS across to last 2 sts, TTPS, TKS (*16 lps on hook*);

B. ch 1, [yo, pull through 2 lps on hook] 4 times, ch 1, [yo, pull lp through 2 lps on hook] 6 times, ch 1, [yo, pull through 2 lps on hook] 5 times.

Rows 7–9: Rep row 6.

Rows 10–104: [Rep rows 5–9 consecutively] 19 times.

Rows 105 & 106: Rep rows 5 and 6.

Row 107:

A. Sk first vertical bar, TTPS, TKS across to last 2 sts, TTPS, TKS (*16 lps on hook*);

B. ch 1, [yo, pull through 2 lps on hook] across.

Last row: Sk first vertical bar, insert hook in next st as for TTPS, yo, pull lp through st and through lp on hook (*sl st made*), sl st as for TKS across to last 2 sts, sl st as for TTPS in next st, sl st as for TKS in last st. Fasten off.

FINISHING

With tapestry needle, seam first row to last row, forming ring.

If desired, completely immerse project in cool water, squeeze lightly, roll in clean towel to remove excess water, lay flat, shape and allow to air dry. ■

SKILL LEVEL

INTERMEDIATE

FINISHED SIZES

5 inches wide x 5 inches high at widest points, flat, after assembly

MATERIALS
- Berroco Vintage DK light (DK) weight yarn (3½ oz/288 yds/100g per hank): 1 hank #2107 cracked pepper
- Size I/9/5.5mm Tunisian crochet hook, minimum length of 10 inches, or size needed to obtain gauge
- Size G/6/4mm crochet hook
- Tapestry needle

GAUGE
Size I hook: 14 TKS = 4 inches; 14 TKS rows = 4 inches

PATTERN NOTES
Project made flat and seamed at back.

Ribbing attached after completion.

Project will curl at bottom edge until ribbing is attached.

See Introduction for information on "mirror image" for left-handed crocheters.

Last loop on hook is counted as first loop of next row unless otherwise stated.

This project uses both Right-Leaning 4-stitch cables (RLC) and Left-Leaning 4-stitch cables (LLC). See pages 7 and 8 for detailed instructions.

SPECIAL STITCH
Increase (inc): Insert hook in top bar of horizontal closing ch between sts, yo, pull lp through.

MITTS
FIRST MITT
Row 1:

A. With size I hook, ch 30, work **typical foundation** *(see page 4)* across *(30 lps on hook)*;

B. ch 1, [yo, pull through 2 lps on hook] across, leaving **last lp on hook** *(see Pattern Notes)*.

Row 2:

A. Sk first vertical bar, 5 **TKS** *(see page 4)*, **TTPS** *(see page 5)*, 8 TKS, TTPS, 14 TKS *(30 lps on hook)*;

B. ch 1, [yo, pull through 2 lps on hook] across.

Row 3: Rep row 2.

Row 4:

A. Sk first vertical bar, 5 TKS, TTPS, 8 TKS, TTPS, 14 TKS *(30 lps on hook)*;

B. ch 1, [yo, pull through 2 lps on hook] 14 times, **RLC** *(see page 7)*, **LLC** *(see page 8)*, [yo, pull through 2 lps on hook] 7 times.

Row 5: When creating all following rows, ignore the ch-1 sp in the center of each cable:

A. Sk first vertical bar, 5 TKS, TTPS, 8 TKS, TTPS, 14 TKS *(30 lps on hook)*;

B. ch 1, [yo, pull through 2 lps on hook] 16 times, ch 1, [yo, pull through 2 lps on hook] 4 times, ch 1, [yo, pull through 2 lps on hook] 9 times.

Row 6: Rep row 5.

Row 7:

A. Sk first vertical bar, 5 TKS, TTPS, 8 TKS, TTPS, 14 TKS *(30 lps on hook)*;

B. ch 1, [yo, pull through 2 lps on hook] 14 times, LLC, RLC, [yo, pull through 2 lps on hook] 7 times.

Row 8:

A. Sk first vertical bar, **inc** *(see Special Stitch)*, 5 TKS, TTPS, 8 TKS, TTPS, 14 TKS *(31 lps on hook)*;

B. ch 1, [yo, pull through 2 lps on hook] 16 times, ch 1, [yo, pull through 2 lps on hook] 4 times,

MANCHESTER
Mitts

ch 1, [yo, pull through 2 lps on hook] 10 times.

Row 9:

A. Sk first vertical bar, inc, 6 TKS, TTPS, 8 TKS, TTPS, 14 TKS *(32 lps on hook)*;

B. ch 1, [yo, pull through 2 lps on hook] 16 times, ch 1, [yo, pull through 2 lps on hook] 4 times, ch 1, [yo, pull through 2 lps on hook] 11 times.

Row 10:

A. Sk first vertical bar, inc, 7 TKS, TTPS, 8 TKS, TTPS, 14 TKS *(33 lps on hook)*;

B. ch 1, [yo, pull through 2 lps on hook] 14 times, LLC, RLC, [yo, pull through 2 lps on hook] 10 times.

Row 11:

A. Sk first vertical bar, inc, 8 TKS, TTPS, 8 TKS, TTPS, 14 TKS *(34 lps on hook)*;

B. ch 1, [yo, pull through 2 lps on hook] 16 times, ch 1, [yo, pull through 2 lps on hook] 4 times, ch 1, [yo, pull through 2 lps on hook] 13 times.

Row 12:

A. Sk first vertical bar, inc, 9 TKS, TTPS, 8 TKS, TTPS, 14 TKS *(35 lps on hook)*;

B. ch 1, [yo, pull through 2 lps on hook] 16 times, ch 1, [yo, pull through 2 lps on hook] 4 times, ch 1, [yo, pull through 2 lps on hook] 14 times.

Row 13:

A. Sk first vertical bar, inc, 10 TKS, TTPS, 8 TKS, TTPS, 14 TKS *(36 lps on hook)*;

B. ch 1, [yo, pull through 2 lps on hook] 14 times, RLC, LLC, [yo, pull through 2 lps on hook] 13 times.

Row 14:

A. Sk first vertical bar, 11 TKS, TTPS, 8 TKS, TTPS, 14 TKS *(36 lps on hook)*;

B. ch 1, [yo, pull through 2 lps on hook] 16 times, ch 1, [yo, pull through 2 lps on hook] 4 times, ch 1, [yo, pull through 2 lps on hook] 15 times.

Row 15: Rep row 14.

Row 16:

A. Sk first vertical bar, 11 TKS, TTPS, 8 TKS, TTPS, 14 TKS *(36 lps on hook)*;

B. ch 1, [yo, pull through 2 lps on hook] 14 times, RLC, LLC, [yo, pull through 2 lps on hook] 13 times.

Row 17:

A. Sk first vertical bar, *insert hook under front vertical bar of next st and under top horizontal bar of next closing ch at same time, yo, pull lp through and pull through 1 lp on hook *(sl st made)*, rep from * 9 times, TKS, TTPS, 8 TKS, TTPS, 14 TKS *(26 lps on hook)*;

B. ch 1, [yo, pull through 2 lps on hook] 16 times , ch 1, [yo, pull through 2 lps on hook] 4 times, ch 1, [yo, pull through 2 lps on hook] 5 times.

Row 18:

A. Sk first vertical bar, TKS, TTPS, 8 TKS, TTPS, 14 TKS *(26 lps on hook)*;

B. ch 1, [yo, pull through 2 lps on hook] 16 times, ch 1, [yo, pull through 2 lps on hook] 4 times, ch 1, [yo, pull through 2 lps on hook] 5 times.

Row 19:

A. Sk first vertical bar, TKS, TTPS, 8 TKS, TTPS, 14 TKS *(26 lps on hook)*;

B. ch 1, [yo, pull through 2 lps on hook] 14 times, LLC, RLC, [yo, pull through 2 lps on hook] 3 times.

Row 20:

A. Sk first vertical bar, TKS, TTPS, 8 TKS, TTPS, 14 TKS (*26 lps on hook*);

B. ch 1, [yo, pull through 2 lps on hook] 16 times, ch 1, [yo, pull through 2 lps on hook] 4 times, ch 1, [yo, pull through 2 lps on hook] 5 times.

Row 21:

A. Sk first vertical bar, TKS, TTPS, 8 TKS, TTPS, 14 TKS (*26 lps on hook*);

B. ch 1, [yo, pull through 2 lps on hook] across.

Last row: Sk first vertical bar, *insert hook under front vertical bar of next st and under top horizontal bar of next closing ch at same time, yo, pull lp through and pull through lp on hook (*sl st made*), rep from * across to last st, sl st as for TKS in last st. Fasten off.

RIBBING

Getting Started: The ribbing is worked vertically along the wrist portion, attaching each row to the Mitt in a join-as-you-go fashion. With sl st, there is no ch-1 at the beg of rows.

Do not work in joining sl sts that are worked into Mitt.

Row 1: With size G hook, ch 4, turn Mitt to beg working in starting ch on opposite side of first row on Mitt, sl st to first ch, turn.

Row 2: Working in back bars of ch, sl st in back bar of each ch across, turn. (*4 sts*)

Row 3: Working **back lps** (*see Stitch Guide*), sl st in each sl st across, **sk joining sl st** (*see Getting Started*), sl st in next ch on Mitt, turn.

Row 4: Working in back lps, sl st in each sl st across, turn.

Next rows: Rep rows 3 and 4 alternately across all chs of first row on Mitt. At end of last row, fasten off.

FINISHING
See page 6 for finishing instructions.

2ND MITT
Row 1:

A. With size I hook, ch 30, work typical foundation across (*30 lps on hook*);

B. ch 1, [yo, pull through 2 lps on hook] across, leaving last lp on hook.

Row 2:

A. Sk first vertical bar, 13 TKS, TTPS, 8 TKS, TTPS, 6 TKS (*30 lps on hook*);

B. ch 1, [yo, pull through 2 lps on hook] across.

Row 3: Rep row 2.

Row 4:

A. Sk first vertical bar, 13 TKS, TTPS, 8 TKS, TTPS, 6 TKS (*30 lps on hook*);

B. ch 1, [yo, pull through 2 lps on hook] 6 times, RLC, LLC, [yo, pull through 2 lps on hook] 15 times.

Row 5: When creating all following rows, ignore the ch-1 sp in the center of each cable:

A. Sk first vertical bar, 13 TKS, TTPS, 8 TKS, TTPS, 6 TKS (*30 lps on hook*);

B. ch 1, [yo, pull through 2 lps on hook] 8 times, ch 1, [yo, pull through 2 lps on hook] 4 times, ch 1, [yo, pull through 2 lps on hook] 17 times.

Row 6: Rep row 5.

Row 7:

A. Sk first vertical bar, 13 TKS, TTPS, 8 TKS, TTPS, 6 TKS (*30 lps on hook*);

B. ch 1, [yo, pull through 2 lps on hook] 6 times, LLC, RLC, [yo, pull through 2 lps on hook] 15 times.

Row 8:

A. Sk first vertical bar, 13 TKS, TTPS, 8 TKS, TTPS, 5 TKS, inc, TKS *(31 lps on hook);*

B. ch 1, [yo, pull through 2 lps on hook] 9 times, ch 1, [yo, pull through 2 lps on hook] 4 times, ch 1, [yo, pull through 2 lps on hook] 17 times.

Row 9:

A. Sk first vertical bar, 13 TKS, TTPS, 8 TKS, TTPS, 6 TKS, inc, TKS *(32 lps on hook);*

B. ch 1, [yo, pull through 2 lps on hook] 10 times, ch 1, [yo, pull through 2 lps on hook] 4 times, ch 1, [yo, pull through 2 lps on hook] 17 times.

Row 10:

A. Sk first vertical bar, 13 TKS, TTPS, 8 TKS, TTPS, 7 TKS, inc, TKS *(33 lps on hook);*

B. ch 1, [yo, pull through 2 lps on hook] 9 times, LLC, RLC, [yo, pull through 2 lps on hook] 15 times.

Row 11:

A. Sk first vertical bar, 13 TKS, TTPS, 8 TKS, TTPS, 8 TKS, inc, TKS *(34 lps on hook);*

B. ch 1, [yo, pull through 2 lps on hook] 12 times, ch 1, [yo, pull through 2 lps on hook] 4 times, ch 1, [yo, pull through 2 lps on hook] 17 times.

Row 12:

A. Sk first vertical bar, 13 TKS, TTPS, 8 TKS, TTPS, 9 TKS, inc, TKS *(35 lps on hook);*

B. ch 1, [yo, pull through 2 lps on hook] 13 times, ch 1, [yo, pull through 2 lps on hook] 4 times, ch 1, [yo, pull through 2 lps on hook] 17 times.

Row 13:

A. Sk first vertical bar, 13 TKS, TTPS, 8 TKS, TTPS, 10 TKS, inc, TKS *(36 lps on hook);*

B. ch 1, [yo, pull through 2 lps on hook] 12 times, RLC, LLC, [yo, pull through 2 lps on hook] 15 times.

Row 14:

A. Sk first vertical bar, 13 TKS, TTPS, 8 TKS, TTPS, 12 TKS *(36 lps on hook);*

B. ch 1, [yo, pull through 2 lps on hook] 14 times, ch 1, [yo, pull through 2 lps on hook] 4 times, ch 1, [yo, pull through 2 lps on hook], 17 times.

Row 15: Rep row 14.

Row 16:

A. Sk first vertical bar, 13 TKS, TTPS, 8 TKS, TTPS, 12 TKS *(36 lps on hook);*

B. ch 1, [yo, pull through 2 lps on hook] 12 times, RLC, LLC, [yo, pull through 2 lps on hook] 15 times.

Row 17:

A. Sk first vertical bar, 13 TKS, TTPS, 8 TKS, TTPS, 3 TKS *(27 lps currently on hook),* *insert hook under front vertical bar of next st and under top horizontal bar of next closing ch at same time, yo, pull lp through and pull through 1 lp on hook *(sl st made),* rep from * across to last st, work sl st as for TKS in last st. Fasten off last st *(26 lps rem on hook);*

B. pull new yarn through first lp *(closing first st),* [yo, pull through 2 lps on hook] 4 times, ch 1, [yo, pull through 2 lps on hook] 4 times, ch 1, [yo, pull through 2 lps on hook] 17 times.

Row 18:

A. Sk first vertical bar, 13 TKS, TTPS, 8 TKS, TTPS, 2 TKS *(26 lps on hook);*

B. ch 1, [yo, pull through 2 lps on hook] 4 times,

ch 1, [yo, pull through 2 lps on hook] 4 times,
ch 1, [yo, pull through 2 lps on hook] 17 times.

Row 19:

A. Sk first vertical bar, 13 TKS, TTPS, 8 TKS, TTPS, 2 TKS *(26 lps on hook)*;

B. ch 1, [yo, pull through 2 lps on hook] 2 times, LLC, RLC, [yo, pull through 2 lps on hook] 15 times.

Row 20:

A. Sk first vertical bar, 13 TKS, TTPS, 8 TKS, TTPS, 2 TKS *(26 lps on hook)*;

B. ch 1, [yo, pull through 2 lps on hook] 4 times, ch 1, [yo, pull through 2 lps on hook] 4 times, ch 1, [yo, pull through 2 lps on hook] 17 times.

Row 21:

A. Sk first vertical bar, 13 TKS, TTPS, 8 TKS, TTPS, 2 TKS *(26 lps on hook)*;

B. ch 1, [yo, pull through 2 lps on hook] across.

Last row: Sk first vertical bar, *insert hook under front vertical bar of next st and under top horizontal bar of next closing ch at same time, yo, pull lp through and pull through lp on hook *(sl st made)*, rep from * across to last st, work sl st as for TKS in last st. Fasten off.

RIBBING

Getting Started: The ribbing is worked vertically along the wrist portion, attaching each row to the Mitt in a join-as-you-go fashion. With sl st, there is no ch-1 at the beg of rows.

Do not work in joining sl sts that are worked into Mitt.

Row 1: With size G hook, ch 4, turn Mitt to beg working in starting ch on opposite side of first row on Mitt, sl st to first ch, turn.

Row 2: Working in back bars of ch, sl st in back bar of each ch across, turn. *(4 sts)*

Row 3: Working in **back lps** *(see Stitch Guide)*, sl st in each sl st across, **sk joining sl st** *(see Getting Started)*, sl st in next ch on Mitt, turn.

Row 4: Working in back lps, sl st in each sl st across, turn.

Next rows: Rep rows 3 and 4 alternately across all chs of first row on Mitt. At end of last row, fasten off.

FINISHING

See page 6 for finishing instructions.

If desired, completely immerse project in cool water, squeeze lightly, roll in clean towel to remove excess water, lie flat, shape and allow to air dry. ∎

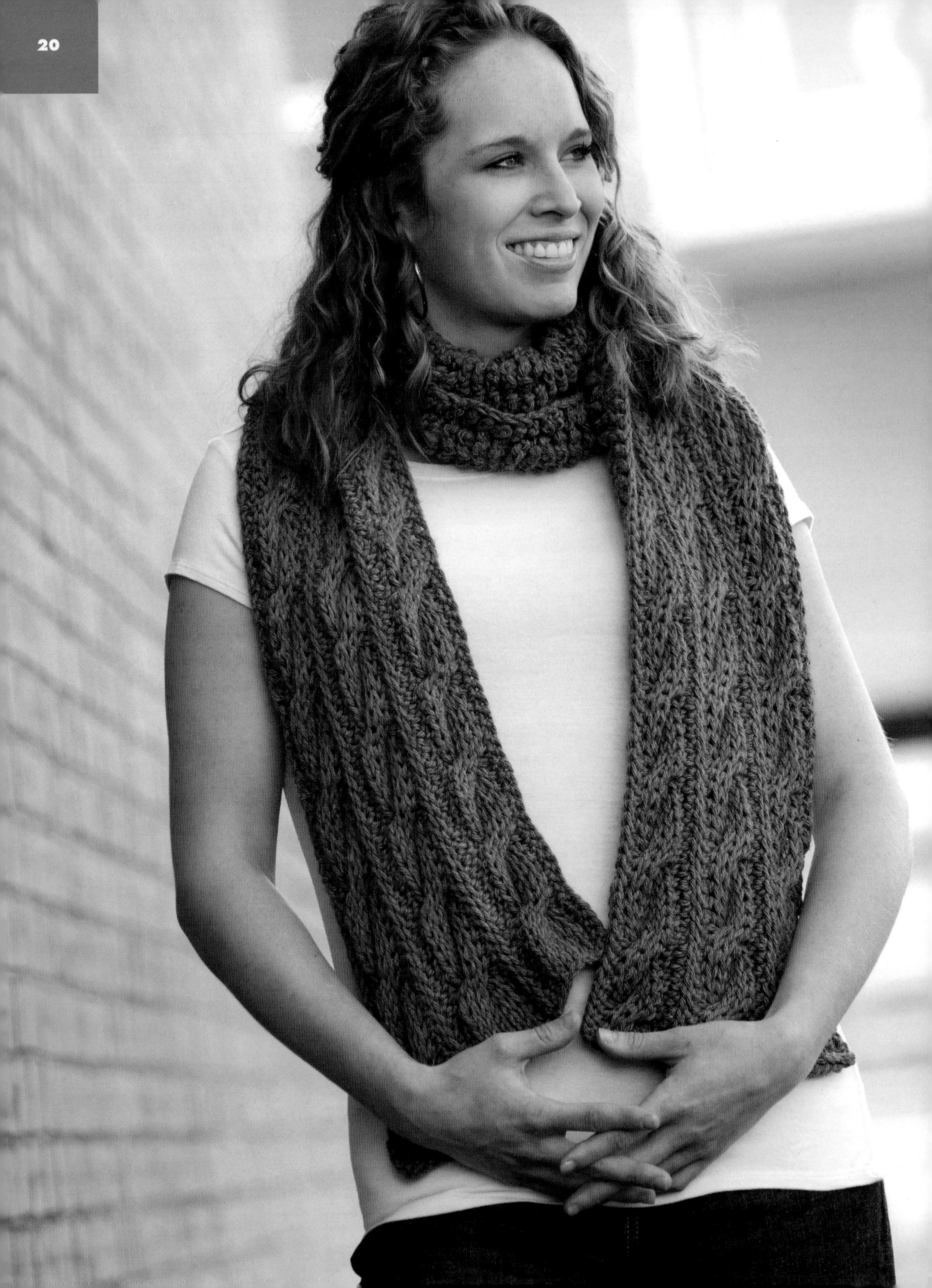

SKILL LEVEL

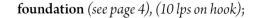

INTERMEDIATE

FINISHED SIZE
8 x 68 inches

MATERIALS
- Berroco Vintage Chunky bulky (chunky) weight yarn (3½ oz/130 yds/100g per hank):
  3 hanks #6183 lilacs
  2 hanks #61190 cerulean
- Size L/11/8mm Tunisian crochet hook, minimum length of 6 inches, or size needed to obtain gauge
- Size I/9/5.5mm crochet hook

GAUGE
Size L hook (after blocking): 10-inch cable section = 2½ inches wide; 8 rows = 3 inches high

PATTERN NOTES
Project made by making first Cable Stitch Strip. The next Cable Stitch Strips are made in a join-as-you-go method.

See Introduction for information on "mirror image" for left-handed crocheters.

Last loop on hook is counted as first loop of next row unless otherwise stated.

This project uses Right-Leaning 6-stitch cables (RLC). See pages 7 and 8 for detailed instructions.

SCARF
FIRST CABLE STRIP
Row 1:

A. With size L hook and lilacs, ch 10, work **typical foundation** *(see page 4)*, *(10 lps on hook)*;

B. ch 1, [yo, pull through 2 lps on hook] across, **1 lp rem on hook** *(see Pattern Notes)*.

Row 2:

A. Sk first vertical bar, **TTPS** *(see page 5)*, **TKS** *(see page 4)* across to last 2 sts, TTPS, TKS *(10 lps on hook)*;

B. ch 1, [yo, pull through 2 lps on hook] across.

Rows 3–6: Rep row 2.

Row 7:

A. Sk first vertical bar, TTPS, TKS across to last 2 sts, TTPS, TKS *(10 lps on hook)*;

B. ch 1, yo, pull through 2 lps on hook, **RLC** *(see Cable)*, [yo, pull through 2 lps on hook] twice.

Row 8: When creating all following rows, ignore the ch-1 sp in the center of each cable:

A. Sk first vertical bar, TTPS, TKS across to last 2 sts, TTPS, TKS *(10 lps on hook)*;

B. ch 1, [yo, pull through 2 lps on hook] 4 times, ch 1, [yo, pull through 2 lps on hook] 5 times.

Rows 9–12: Rep row 8.

Rows 13–174: [Rep rows 7–12 consecutively] 27 times.

Rows 175 & 176: Rep rows 7 and 8.

Row 177:

A. Sk first vertical bar, TTPS, TKS across to last 2 sts, TTPS, TKS (*10 lps on hook*);

B. ch 1, [yo, pull through 2 lps on hook] across.

Last row: Sk first vertical bar, insert hook in next st as for TTPS, yo, pull lp through st and through lp on hook (*sl st made*), sl st as for TKS across to last 2 sts, sl st as for TTPS in next st, sl st as for TKS in last st. Fasten off.

2ND CABLE STRIP

Row 1:

A. With size L hook and cerulean, ch 10, work typical foundation across to last ch, insert hook in back bar of last ch and in back vertical bar of first st of row 1 of First Cable Strip, yo, pull lp through both sts at same time (*10 lps on hook*);

B. there is no ch-1 at the beg of joining row, [yo, pull through 2 lps on hook] across.

Row 2:

A. Sk first vertical bar, TTPS, TKS across to last 2 sts, TTPS, insert hook in last st as for **TSS** (*see page 4*) and in back vertical bar of first st of next row of First Cable Strip, yo, pull lp through both sts at same time (*10 lps on hook*);

B. [yo, pull through 2 lps on hook] across.

Rows 3–6: Rep row 2.

Row 7:

A. Sk first vertical bar, TTPS, TKS across to last 2 sts, TTPS, insert hook in last st as for TSS and in back vertical bar of first st of next row of First Cable Strip, yo, pull lp through both sts at same time (*10 lps on hook*);

B. yo, pull through 2 lps on hook, RLC, [yo, pull through 2 lps on hook] twice.

Row 8: When creating all following rows, ignore the ch-1 sp in the center of each cable:

A. Sk first vertical bar, TTPS, TKS across to last 2 sts, TTPS, insert hook in last st as for TSS and in back vertical bar of first st of next row of First Cable Strip, yo, pull lp through both sts at same time (*10 lps on hook*);

B. [yo, pull through 2 lps on hook] 4 times, ch 1, [yo, pull through 2 lps on hook] 5 times.

Rows 9–12: Rep row 8.

Rows 13–174: [Rep rows 7–12 consecutively] 27 times.

Rows 175 & 176: Rep rows 7 and 8.

Row 177:

A. Sk first vertical bar, TTPS, TKS across to last 2 sts, TTPS, insert hook in last st as for TSS and in back vertical bar of first st of next row of First Cable Strip, yo, pull lp through both sts at same time (*10 lps on hook*);

B. [yo, pull through 2 lps on hook] across.

Last row: Sk first vertical bar, insert hook in next st as for TTPS, yo, pull lp through st and through lp on hook (*sl st made*), sl st as for TKS across to last 2 sts, sl st as for TTPS in next st, insert hook in last st as for TSS and in back vertical bar of first st of next row of First Cable Strip, yo, pull lp through both sts at same time and through last lp on hook. Fasten off.

3RD CABLE STRIP
With lilacs, work same as for 2nd Cable Strip, connecting to 2nd Cable Strip.

FINISHING
If desired, completely immerse project in cool water, squeeze lightly, roll in clean towel to remove excess water, lay flat, shape and allow to air dry. ■

VERONA
Ruana

SKILL LEVEL
■■■□
INTERMEDIATE

FINISHED SIZE
After blocking: 29 x 47 inches

MATERIALS
- Plymouth Yarn Baby Alpaca Grande bulky (chunky) weight yarn (3½ oz/110 yds/100g per skein):
  11 skeins #1496 red
- Size L/11/8mm Tunisian crochet hook, minimum length of 20 inches, or size needed to obtain gauge
- Size I/9/5.5mm crochet hook

GAUGE
Size L hook after blocking: 11 pattern sts = 4 inches; 11 pattern rows = 4 inches

Alpaca grows significantly when wet, so blocked gauge is given.

PATTERN NOTES
Project is made in 1 piece, beginning at hem of back, working up to shoulders, splitting at neck, where 2 fronts are worked separately and is completed at the front hem.

See Introduction for information on "mirror image" for left-handed crocheters.

This project does not use a typical foundation row.

Last loop on hook is counted as first loop of next row unless otherwise stated.

This project uses both Right-Leaning 6-stitch cables (RLC) and Left-Leaning 6-stitch cables (LLC). See pages 7 and 8 for detailed instructions.

SPECIAL STITCH

Increase (inc): Insert hook in top bar of horizontal closing ch between sts, yo, pull lp through.

RUANA
Row 1:

    A. With size L hook, ch 81, working in **back bar of chain** *(see page 4)* and holding back all lps on hook, insert hook in 3rd ch from hook, yo, pull lp through, ch 1, [insert hook in next ch, yo, pull lp through, ch 1] in each ch across *(80 lps on hook)*;

    B. ch 1, [yo, pull through 2 lps on hook] across, **1 lp rem on hook** *(see Pattern Notes)*.

Row 2:

    A. Sk first vertical bar, **TKS** *(see page 4)* across *(80 lps on hook)*;

    B. ch 1, [yo, pull through 2 lps on hook] across.

Rows 3 & 4: Rep row 2.

Row 5:

    A. Sk first vertical bar, TKS across *(80 lps on hook)*;

    B. ch 1, *RLC *(see page 7)*, [yo, pull through 2 lps on hook] 6 times, rep from * across to last 7 sts *(8 lps rem on hook)*, RLC, yo, pull through 2 lps on hook.

Row 6: When creating all following rows, ignore the ch-1 sp in the center of each cable, even when the cable has not yet been started:

    A. Sk first vertical bar, TKS across *(80 lps on hook)*;

    B. ch 1, [yo, pull through 2 lps on hook] 3 times, *ch 1, [yo, pull through 2 lps on hook] 6 times, rep from * across to last 4 sts, ch 1, [yo, pull through 2 lps on hook] 4 times.

Rows 7 & 8: Rep row 6.

Row 9:

    A. Sk first vertical bar, TKS across *(80 lps on hook)*;

    B. ch 1, *[yo, pull through 2 lps on hook] 6 times, LLC *(see page 8)*, rep from * across to last 7 sts *(8 lps rem on hook)*, [yo, pull through 2 lps on hook] 7 times.

Row 10:

    A. Sk first vertical bar, TKS across *(80 lps on hook)*;

    B. ch 1, [yo, pull through 2 lps on hook] 3 times, *ch 1, [yo, pull through 2 lps on hook] 6 times, rep from * across to last 4 sts, ch 1, [yo, pull through 2 lps on hook] 4 times.

Rows 11 & 12: Rep row 10.

Rows 13–68: [Rep rows 5–12 consecutively] 7 times.

FIRST FRONT
Row 69:

    A. Sk first vertical bar, 36 TKS, [**inc** *(see Special Stitch)*, TKS] 4 times *(44 lps on hook)*, leave rem sts unworked;

    B. ch 1, *RLC, [yo, pull through 2 lps on hook] 6 times, rep from * across to last 7 sts *(8 lps rem on hook)*, RLC, yo, pull through 2 lps on hook.

Rows 70–76: Rep rows 6–12.

Rows 77–116: [Rep rows 5–12 consecutively] 5 times.

Rows 117–123: Rep rows 5–11.

Row 124:

A. Sk first vertical bar, TKS across *(44 lps on hook)*;

B. ch 1, [yo, pull through 2 lps on hook] across.

Row 125:

A. Ch 1, sk first vertical bar, **TES** *(see page 6)* across *(44 lps on hook)*;

B. ch 1, [yo, pull through 2 lps hook] across.

Row 126: Rep row 124.

Last row: Sk first vertical bar, insert hook in next st as for TKS, yo, pull lp through st and through lp on hook *(sl st made)*, sl st as for TKS across. Fasten off.

2ND FRONT
Row 69: Working across unworked sts from row 68:

A. Pull lp through first unworked st, [inc, TKS] 4 times, TKS across rem unworked sts *(44 lps on hook)*;

B. ch 1, *RLC, [yo, pull through 2 lps on hook] 6 times, rep from * across to last 7 sts *(8 lps rem on hook)*, RLC, yo, pull through 2 lps on hook.

Rows 70–last row: Rep rows 70–last row same as for First Front.

FINISHING
If desired, completely immerse project in cool water, squeeze lightly, roll in clean towel to remove excess water, lie flat, shape and allow to air dry. ■

VIENNA
Hat & Scarf

SKILL LEVEL
INTERMEDIATE

FINISHED SIZES
Hat: 8 inches high x 19 inches circumference; stretches to fit up to 23 inches circumference

Scarf: 7 x 66 inches

MATERIALS
- Premier Yarns Alpaca Dance medium (worsted) weight yarn (3½ oz/371 yds/100g per skein):
  3 skeins #17 wood nymph
- Size I/9/5.5mm Tunisian crochet hook, minimum length of 10 inches, or size needed to obtain gauge
- Size G/6/4mm crochet hook
- Tapestry needle
- Stitch markers

GAUGE
Size I hook: 17 pattern sts = 4 inches; 13 pattern st rows = 4 inches

PATTERN NOTES
Ribbing is worked last.

Item will curl at bottom until trim or ribbing is worked.

See Introduction for information on "mirror image" for left-handed crocheters.

Last loop on hook is counted as first loop of next row unless otherwise stated.

Join with slip stitch as indicated unless otherwise stated.

These projects use both Right-Leaning 4-stitch cables (RLC) and Left-Leaning 4-stitch cables (LLC). See pages 7 and 8 for detailed instructions.

SPECIAL STITCH

Decrease (dec): Insert hook as for TKS in 2 sts at same time, yo, pull lp through.

HAT

Getting Started: Project made flat and seamed at back. Ribbing attached after completion. Project will curl at bottom until trim/ribbing is attached.

Row 1:

A. With size I hook, ch 90, work **typical foundation** *(see page 4) (90 lps on hook)*;

B. ch 1, [yo, pull through 2 lps on hook] across, leaving **last lp on hook** *(see Pattern Notes)*.

Row 2:

A. Sk first vertical bar, **TKS** *(see page 4)* across *(90 lps on hook)*;

B. ch 1, [yo, pull through 2 lps on hook] across.

Row 3:

A. Sk first vertical bar, TKS across *(90 lps on hook)*;

B. ch 1, [**RLC** *(see page 7)*, **LLC** *(see page 8)*] 11 times, yo, pull through 2 lps on hook.

Row 4: When creating all following rows, ignore ch-1 sp in center of each cable:

A. Sk first vertical bar, TKS across *(90 lps on hook)*;

B. ch 1, [yo, pull through 2 lps on hook] twice, *ch 1, [yo, pull through 2 lps on hook] 4 times, rep from * 20 times, [yo, pull through 2 lps on hook] 3 times.

Row 5: Rep row 4.

Row 6:

A. Sk first vertical bar, TKS across *(90 lps on hook)*;

B. ch 1, [LLC, RLC] 11 times, yo, pull through last 2 lps on hook.

Rows 7 & 8: Rep row 4.

Rows 9–14: Rep rows 3–8.

Row 15: Rep row 3.

Row 16:

A. Sk first vertical bar, **dec** *(see Special Stitch)*, TKS across *(89 lps on hook)*;

B. ch 1, [yo, pull through 2 lps on hook] across.

Row 17:

A. Sk first vertical bar, [dec, 9 TKS] 8 times *(81 lps on hook)*;

B. ch 1, [yo, pull through 2 lps on hook] across.

Row 18:

A. Sk first vertical bar, [dec, 8 TKS] 8 times *(73 lps on hook)*;

B. ch 1, [yo, pull through 2 lps on hook] across.

Row 19:

A. Sk first vertical bar, [dec, 7 TKS] 8 times *(65 lps on hook)*;

B. ch 1, [yo, pull through 2 lps on hook] across.

Row 20:

A. Sk first vertical bar, [dec, 6 TKS] 8 times *(57 lps on hook)*;

B. ch 1, [yo, pull through 2 lps on hook] across.

Row 21:

A. Sk first vertical bar, [dec, 5 TKS] 8 times *(49 lps on hook)*;

B. ch 1, [yo, pull through 2 lps on hook] across.

Row 22:

A. Sk first vertical bar, [dec, 4 TKS] 8 times *(41 lps on hook)*;

B. ch 1, [yo, pull through 2 lps on hook] across.

Row 23:

A. Sk first vertical bar, [dec, 3 TKS] 8 times *(33 lps on hook)*;

B. ch 1, [yo, pull through 2 lps on hook] across.

Row 24:

A. Sk first vertical bar, [dec, 2 TKS] 8 times *(25 lps on hook)*;

B. ch 1, [yo, pull through 2 lps on hook] across.

Row 25:

A. Sk first vertical bar, [dec, TKS] 8 times *(17 lps on hook)*;

B. ch 1, [yo, pull through 2 lps on hook] across.

Row 26:

A. Sk first vertical bar, dec 8 times *(9 lps on hook)*;

B. ch 1, [yo, pull through 2 lps on hook] across.

Row 27:

A. Sk first vertical bar, dec 4 times *(5 lps on hook)*;

B. yo and pull through all 5 lps. Fasten off.

RIBBING
Getting Started: The Ribbing is worked vertically in starting ch on opposite side of row 1 of Hat, attaching each row to the Hat in a join-as-you-go fashion. With sl st, there is no ch 1 at the beg of rows.

Do not work in sl sts that are worked into Hat.

With st markers or small contrasting pieces of yarn, mark 8 evenly spaced sts in row 1 of Hat.

Row 1: With size G hook, ch 5, sl st to first ch of row 1 of Hat, turn.

Row 2: Sl st in back bar of each ch across, turn. *(5 sts)*

Row 3: Sl st in **back lp** *(see Stitch Guide)* of each sl st, sk sl st where joined to Hat, sl st in next ch in row 1 of Hat, turn.

Row 4: Sk last sl st worked, sl st in back lp of each sl st across, turn. *(5 sl sts)*

Next rows: Rep rows 3 and 4 alternately across chs of row 1 on Hat, sk all marked sts. Fasten off.

FINISHING
See page 6 for finishing instructions.

If desired, completely immerse project in cool water, squeeze lightly, roll in clean towel to remove excess water, lie flat, shape and allow to air dry.

SCARF
Getting Started: Trim applied after completion.

Project will curl at the bottom until trim/ribbing is applied.

Row 1:

A. With size I hook, ch 30, work **typical foundation** *(see page 4)* *(30 lps on hook)*;

B. ch 1, [yo, pull through 2 lps on hook] across, leaving **last lp on hook** *(see Pattern Notes)*.

Row 2:

A. Sk first vertical bar, 2 **TTPS** *(see page 5)*, **TKS** *(see page 4)* across to last 3 sts, 2 TTPS,

TKS *(30 lps on hook)*;

B. ch 1, [yo, pull through 2 lps on hook] across.

Row 3:

A. Sk first vertical bar, 2 TTPS, TKS across to last 3 sts, 2 TTPS, TKS *(30 lps on hook)*;

B. ch 1, [yo, pull through 2 lps on hook] twice, [**LLC** *(see page 8)*, **RLC** *(see page 7)*] 3 times, [yo, pull through 2 lps on hook] 3 times.

Row 4: When creating all following rows, ignore the ch-1 sp in the center of each cable:

A. Sk first vertical bar, 2 TTPS, TKS across to last 3 sts, 2 TTPS, TKS *(30 lps on hook)*;

B. ch 1, [yo, pull through 2 lps on hook] 4 times, *ch 1, [yo, pull through 2 lps on hook] 4 times, rep from * 4 times, [yo, pull through 2 lps on hook] 5 times.

Row 5: Rep row 4.

Row 6:

A. Sk first vertical bar, 2 TTPS, TKS across to last 3 sts, 2 TTPS, TKS *(30 lps on hook)*;

B. ch 1, [yo, pull through 2 lps on hook] twice, [RLC, LLC] 3 times, [yo, pull through 2 lps on hook] 3 times.

Rows 7 & 8: Rep row 4.

Rows 9–206: [Rep rows 3–8 consecutively] 33 times.

Rows 207–211: Rep rows 3–7.

Row 212:

A. Sk first vertical bar, 2 TTPS, TKS across to last 3 sts, 2 TTPS, TKS *(30 lps on hook)*;

B. ch 1, [yo, pull through 2 lps on hook] across.

Last row: Sk first vertical bar, [insert hook as for TTPS, yo, pull lp through and pull through lp on hook *(sl st made)*] twice, *sl st as for TKS across to last 3 sts, [sl st as for TTPS] twice, sl st as for TKS in last st. Fasten off.

TRIM
Getting Started: The Trim is worked vertically along the short ends of Scarf, attaching each row to the Scarf in a join-as-you-go fashion. With slip stitch, there is no ch-1 at the beginning of rows.

Do not work in sl sts that are worked into Scarf.

Row 1: With size G hook, ch 8, sl st to first st at 1 short edge of Scarf, turn.

Row 2: Sl st in back bar of each ch across, turn. *(8 sts)*

Row 3: Sk sl st where joined to Scarf, sl st in **back lp** *(see Stitch Guide)* of each of next 8 sl sts, sl st in next st at first row of Scarf, turn.

Row 4: Sl st in back lp of each of next 8 sl sts, turn.

Next rows: Rep rows 3 and 4 across all sts of short edge. At end of last row, fasten off.

Rep Trim on rem opposite short edge of Scarf.

FINISHING
If desired, completely immerse project in cool water, squeeze lightly, roll in clean towel to remove excess water, lie flat, shape and allow to air dry. ∎

SKILL LEVEL

INTERMEDIATE

FINISHED SIZES

Hat: 7½ x 18 inches, stretches to fit up to 22 inch circumference

Mitts: 5 inches wide x 5 inches long at widest points, flat, after assembly

MATERIALS

- Plymouth Yarn DK Merino Superwash light (DK) weight yarn (1¾ oz/130 yds/50g per skein):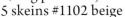
    5 skeins #1102 beige
- Size I/9/5.5mm Tunisian crochet hook, minimum length of 10 inches, or size needed to obtain gauge
- Size G/6/4mm crochet hook
- Tapestry needle
- Sewing needle
- Sewing thread to match
- 5/16-inch round buttons:
    4 buttons for mitts
    12 buttons for hat
- Stitch markers

GAUGE

Size I hook: 14 TKS = 4 inches; 14 TKS rows = 4 inches

PATTERN NOTES

Project made flat and sewed at back.

Ribbing attached after completion.

Project will curl at bottom edge until ribbing is attached.

See Introduction for information on "mirror image" for left-handed crocheters.

Last loop on hook is counted as first loop of next row unless otherwise stated.

Join with slip stitch as indicated unless otherwise stated.

This project uses both Right-Leaning 4-stitch cables (RLC) and Left-Leaning 4-stitch cables (LLC). See pages 7 and 8 for detailed instructions.

SPECIAL STITCHES

Decrease (dec): Insert hook as for TKS in 2 sts at same time, yo, pull lp through.

Increase (inc): Insert hook in top bar of horizontal closing ch between sts, yo, pull lp through.

HAT

Getting Started: Project made flat and seamed at back.

Ribbing attached after completion. Project will curl at bottom until ribbing is worked.

Row 1:

A. With size I hook, ch 85, work **typical foundation** (*see page 4*) across (*85 lps on hook*);

B. ch 1, [yo, pull through 2 lps on hook] across, leaving **last lp on hook** (*see Pattern Notes*).

Row 2:

A. Sk first vertical bar, **TKS** (*see page 4*), [2 **TTPS** (*see page 5*),

DUBLIN OWL
Hat & Mitts

8 TKS, 2 TTPS, 2 TKS] 5 times, 2 TTPS, 8 TKS, 2 TTPS, TKS *(85 lps on hook)*;

B. ch 1, [yo, pull through 2 lps on hook] across.

Row 3: Rep row 2.

Row 4:

A. Sk first vertical bar, [2 TTPS, 8 TKS, 2 TTPS, 2 TKS] 5 times, 2 TTPS, 8 TKS, 2 TTPS, TKS *(85 lps on hook)*;

B. ch 1, [yo, pull through 2 lps on hook] twice, **LLC *(see page 8)*, **RLC** *(see page 7)*, [yo, pull through 2 lps on hook] 6 times, rep from * 4 times, LLC, RLC, [yo, pull through 2 lps on hook] 4 times.

Row 5: When creating all following rows, ignore ch-1 sp in the center of each cable:

A. Sk first vertical bar, [2 TTPS, 8 TKS, 2 TTPS, 2 TKS] 5 times, 2 TTPS, 8 TKS, 2 TTPS, TKS *(85 lps on hook)*;

B. ch 1, [yo, pull through 2 lps on hook] 4 times, **ch 1, [yo, pull through 2 lps on hook] 4 times, ch 1, [yo, pull through 2 lps on hook] 10 times, rep from * 4 times, ch 1, [yo, pull through 2 lps on hook] 4 times, ch 1, [yo, pull through 2 lps on hook] 6 times.

Rows 6–9: Rep row 5.

Row 10: Rep row 4.

Rows 11 & 12: Rep row 5.

Row 13: Rep row 4.

Row 14: Rep row 5.

Row 15:

A. Sk first vertical bar, [2 TTPS, 8 TKS, 2 TTPS, 2 TKS] 5 times, 2 TTPS, 8 TKS, 2 TTPS, TKS *(85 lps on hook)*;

B. ch 1, [yo, pull through 2 lps on hook] across.

Row 16:

A. Sk first vertical bar, TKS, [12 TTPS, 2 TKS] 5 times, 12 TTPS, TKS *(85 lps on hook)*;

B. ch 1, [yo, pull through 2 lps on hook] across.

Row 17: Rep row 16.

Row 18:

A. Sk first vertical bar, TKS across *(85 lps on hook)*;

B. ch 1, [yo, pull through 2 lps on hook] across.

Row 19:

A. Sk first vertical bar, [**dec** *(see Special Stitches)*, 12 TKS] across *(79 lps on hook)*;

B. ch 1, [yo, pull through 2 lps on hook] across.

Row 20:

A. Sk first vertical bar, [dec, 11 TKS] across *(73 lps on hook)*;

B. ch 1, [yo, pull through 2 lps on hook] across.

Row 21:

A. Sk first vertical bar, [dec, 10 TKS] across *(67 lps on hook)*;

B. ch 1, [yo, pull through 2 lps on hook] across.

Row 22:

A. Sk first vertical bar, [dec, 9 TKS] across *(61 lps on hook)*;

B. ch 1, [yo, pull through 2 lps on hook] across.

Row 23:

A. Sk first vertical bar, [dec, 8 TKS] across *(55 lps on hook)*;

B. ch 1, [yo, pull through 2 lps on hook] across.

Row 24:

A. Sk first vertical bar, [dec, 7 TKS] across *(49 lps on hook)*;

B. ch 1, [yo, pull through 2 lps on hook] across.

Row 25:

A. Sk first vertical bar, [dec, 6 TKS] across *(43 lps on hook)*;

B. ch 1, [yo, pull through 2 lps on hook] across.

Row 26:

A. Sk first vertical bar, [dec, 5 TKS] across *(37 lps on hook)*;

B. ch 1, [yo, pull through 2 lps on hook] across.

Row 27:

A. Sk first vertical bar, [dec, 4 TKS] across *(31 lps on hook)*;

B. ch 1, [yo, pull through 2 lps on hook] across.

Row 28:

A. Sk first vertical bar, [dec, 3 TKS] across *(25 lps on hook)*;

B. ch 1, [yo, pull through 2 lps on hook] across.

Row 29:

A. Sk first vertical bar, [dec, 2 TKS] across *(19 lps on hook)*;

B. ch 1, [yo, pull through 2 lps on hook] across.

Row 30:

A. Sk first vertical bar, [dec, TKS] across *(13 lps on hook)*;

B. ch 1, [yo, pull through 2 lps on hook] across.

Row 31:

A. Sk first vertical bar, dec across *(7 lps on hook)*;

B. yo and pull through all 7 lps at same time. Fasten off.

RIBBING

Getting Started: The ribbing is worked vertically in starting ch on opposite side of row 1 of Hat, attaching each row to Hat in a join-as-you-go fashion. With sl st, there is no ch-1 at the beginning of rows.

With st markers or small contrasting pieces of yarn, mark 8 evenly spaced sts in starting ch of row 1 of Hat.

Do not work in sl sts that are worked into Hat.

Row 1: With size G hook, ch 5, turn Hat to beg working in starting ch on opposite side of row 1 of Hat, sl st in first ch, turn.

Row 2: Working in back bars of ch, sl st in back bar of each ch across, turn. *(5 sts)*

Row 3: Working in **back lps** *(see Stitch Guide)*, **sk sl sts worked in Hat** *(see Getting Started)*, sl st in each of next 5 sl sts, sl st in next ch on Hat, turn. *(5 sts)*

Row 4: Sl st in back lp only of each of next 5 sl sts, turn.

Next rows: Rep rows 3 and 4 across starting ch and sk each marked st. At end of last row, fasten off.

FINISHING

See page 6 for finishing instructions.

If desired, completely immerse project in cool water, squeeze lightly, roll in clean towel to remove excess water, lie flat, shape and allow to air dry.

With sewing needle and thread, attach buttons as shown in photo.

MITTS
FIRST MITT

Getting Started: Project made flat and seamed at back.

Ribbing attached after completion. Project will curl at bottom until ribbing is worked.

Row 1:

    A. With size I hook, ch 30, work **typical foundation** *(see page 4) (30 lps on hook);*

    B. ch 1, [yo, pull through 2 lps on hook] across, leaving **last lp on hook** *(see Pattern Notes).*

Row 2:

    A. Sk first vertical bar, **TKS** *(see page 4)* across *(30 lps on hook);*

    B. ch 1, [yo, pull through 2 lps on hook] across.

Rows 3 & 4: Rep row 2.

Row 5:

    A. Sk first vertical bar, 5 TKS, **TTPS** *(see page 5)*, 8 TKS, TTPS, 14 TKS *(30 lps on hook);*

    B. ch 1, [yo, pull through 2 lps on hook] 14 times, **LLC** *(see page 8)*, **RLC** *(see page 7)*, [yo, pull through 2 lps on hook] 7 times.

Row 6: When creating all following rows, ignore ch-1 sp in center of each cable:

    A. Sk first vertical bar, 5 TKS, TTPS, 8 TKS, TTPS, 14 TKS *(30 lps on hook);*

    B. ch 1, [yo, pull through 2 lps on hook] 16 times, ch 1, [yo, pull through 2 lps on hook] 4 times, ch 1, [yo, pull through 2 lps on hook] 9 times.

Row 7:

    A. Sk first vertical bar, **inc** *(see Special Stitches)*, 5 TKS, TTPS, 8 TKS, TTPS, 14 TKS *(31 lps on hook);*

    B. ch 1, [yo, pull through 2 lps on hook] 16 times, ch 1, [yo, pull through 2 lps on hook] 4 times, ch 1, [yo, pull through 2 lps on hook] 10 times.

Row 8:

    A. Sk first vertical bar, inc, 6 TKS, TTPS, 8 TKS, TTPS, 14 TKS *(32 lps on hook);*

    B. ch 1, [yo, pull through 2 lps on hook] 16 times, ch 1, [yo, pull through 2 lps on hook] 4 times, ch 1, [yo, pull through 2 lps on hook] 11 times.

Row 9:

    A. Sk first vertical bar, inc, 7 TKS, TTPS, 8 TKS, TTPS, 14 TKS *(33 lps on hook);*

    B. ch 1, [yo, pull through 2 lps on hook] 16 times, ch 1, [yo, pull through 2 lps on hook] 4 times, ch 1, [yo, pull through 2 lps on hook] 12 times.

Row 10:

    A. Sk first vertical bar, inc, 8 TKS, TTPS, 8 TKS, TTPS, 14 TKS *(34 lps on hook);*

    B. ch 1, [yo, pull through 2 lps on hook] 14 times, LLC, RLC, [yo, pull through 2 lps on hook] 11 times.

Row 11:

    A. Sk first vertical bar, inc, 9 TKS, TTPS, 8 TKS, TTPS, 14 TKS *(35 lps on hook);*

    B. ch 1, [yo, pull through 2 lps on hook] 16 times, ch 1, [yo, pull through 2 lps on hook] 4 times, ch 1, [yo, pull through 2 lps on hook] 14 times.

Row 12:

    A. Sk first vertical bar, inc, 10 TKS, TTPS, 8 TKS, TTPS, 14 TKS *(36 lps on hook);*

    B. ch 1, [yo, pull through 2 lps on hook] 16 times, ch 1, [yo, pull through 2 lps on hook] 4 times, ch 1, [yo, pull through 2 lps on hook] 14 times.

Row 13:

- **A.** Sk first vertical bar, *insert hook under front vertical bar of next st and under top horizontal bar of next closing chain at same time, yo, pull lp through and pull through lp on hook *(sl st made)*, rep from * 9 times, TKS, TTPS, 8 TKS, TTPS, 14 TKS *(26 lps on hook)*;

- **B.** ch 1, [yo, pull through 2 lps on hook] 14 times, LLC, RLC, [yo, pull through 2 lps on hook] 3 times.

Row 14:

- **A.** Sk first vertical bar, TKS, TTPS, 8 TKS, TTPS, 14 TKS *(26 lps on hook)*;

- **B.** ch 1, [yo, pull through 2 lps on hook] 16 times, ch 1, [yo, pull through 2 lps on hook] 4 times, ch 1, [yo, pull through 2 lps on hook] 5 times.

Row 15:

- **A.** Sk first vertical bar, TKS across *(26 lps on hook)*;

- **B.** ch 1, [yo, pull through 2 lps on hook] across.

Row 16: Rep row 15.

Last row: Sk first vertical bar, *insert hook under front vertical bar of next st and under top horizontal bar of next closing ch at same time, yo, pull through and pull through lp on hook *(sl st made)*, rep from * across to last st, work sl st as for TKS in last st. Fasten off.

RIBBING
Getting Started: The ribbing is worked vertically along the wrist portion, attaching each row to the Mitt in a join-as-you-go fashion. With sl st, there is no ch-1 at the beg of rows.

Do not work in sl sts that are worked into Mitt.

Row 1: With size G hook, ch 4, turn Mitt to beg working in starting ch on opposite side of row 1 on Mitt, sl st to first ch of first st, turn.

Row 2: Working in back bars of ch, sl st in each

ch across, turn. *(4 sts)*

Row 3: Working in back lps *(see Stitch Guide)*, sl st in each sl st across, **sk sl st worked in Mitt** *(see Getting Started)*, sl st in next ch first row of Mitt, turn.

Row 4: Working in back lps, sl st in each st across, turn.

Next rows: Rep rows 3 and 4 alternately across rem ch of first row of Mitt. At end of last row, fasten off.

FINISHING
See page 6 for finishing instructions.

If desired, completely immerse project in cool water, squeeze lightly, roll in clean towel to remove excess water, lie flat, shape and allow to air dry.

With sewing needle and thread, attach buttons as shown in photo.

2ND MITT
Rows 1–4: Rep rows 1–4 of First Mitt.

Row 5:

- **A.** Sk first vertical bar, 13 TKS, TTPS, 8 TKS, TTPS, 6 TKS *(30 lps on hook)*;

- **B.** ch 1, [yo, pull through 2 lps on hook] 6 times, LLC, RLC, [yo, pull through 2 lps on hook] 15 times.

Row 6: When creating all following rows, ignore the ch-1 sp in the center of each cable:

- **A.** Sk first vertical bar, 13 TKS, TTPS, 8 TKS, TTPS, 6 TKS *(30 lps on hook)*;

- **B.** ch 1, [yo, pull through 2 lps on hook] 6 times, ch 1, [yo, pull through 2 lps on hook] 4 times, ch 1, [yo, pull through 2 lps on hook] 17 times.

Row 7:

- **A.** Sk first vertical bar, 13 TKS, TTPS, 8 TKS, TTPS, 5 TKS, inc, TKS *(31 lps on hook)*;

B. ch 1, [yo, pull through 2 lps on hook] 9 times, ch 1, [yo, pull through 2 lps on hook] 4 times, ch 1, [yo, pull through 2 lps on hook] 17 times.

Row 8:

A. Sk first vertical bar, 13 TKS, TTPS, 8 TKS, TTPS, 6 TKS, inc, TKS (*32 lps on hook*);

B. ch 1, [yo, pull through 2 lps on hook] 10 times, ch 1, [yo, pull through 2 lps on hook] 4 times, ch 1, [yo, pull through 2 lps on hook] 17 times.

Row 9:

A. Sk first vertical bar, 13 TKS, TTPS, 8 TKS, TTPS, 7 TKS, inc, TKS (*33 lps on hook*);

B. ch 1, [yo, pull through 2 lps on hook] 11 times, ch 1, [yo, pull through 2 lps on hook] 4 times, ch 1, [yo, pull through 2 lps on hook] 17 times.

Row 10:

A. Sk first vertical bar, 13 TKS, TTPS, 8 TKS, TTPS, 8 TKS, inc, TKS (*34 lps on hook*);

B. ch 1, [yo, pull through 2 lps on hook] 10 times, LLC, RLC, [yo, pull through 2 lps on hook] 15 times.

Row 11:

A. Sk first vertical bar, 13 TKS, TTPS, 8 TKS, TTPS, 9 TKS, inc, TKS (*35 lps on hook*);

B. ch 1, [yo, pull through 2 lps on hook] 13 times, ch 1, [yo, pull through 2 lps on hook] 4 times, ch 1, [yo, pull through 2 lps on hook] 17 times.

Row 12:

A. Sk first vertical bar, 13 TKS, TTPS, 8 TKS, TTPS, 10 TKS, inc, TKS (*36 lps on hook*);

B. ch 1, [yo, pull through 2 lps on hook] 14 times, ch 1, [yo, pull through 2 lps on hook]

4 times, ch 1, [yo, pull through 2 lps on hook] 17 times.

Row 13:

A. Sk first vertical bar, 13 TKS, TTPS, 8 TKS, TTPS, 3 TKS (*27 lps currently on hook*), *insert hook under front vertical bar of next st and under top horizontal bar of next closing ch at same time, yo, pull lp through and pull through lp on hook (*sl st made*), rep from * across to last st, work sl st as for TKS in last st. Fasten off last st (*26 lps rem on hook*);

B. pull new yarn through first lp (*closing first st*), [yo, pull through 2 lps on hook] twice, LLC, RLC, [yo, pull through 2 lps on hook] 15 times.

Row 14:

A. Sk first vertical bar, 13 TKS, TTPS, 8 TKS, TTPS, 2 TKS (*26 lps on hook*);

B. ch 1, [yo, pull through 2 lps on hook] 4 times, ch 1, [yo, pull through 2 lps on hook] 4 times, ch 1, [yo, pull through 2 lps on hook] 17 times.

Row 15:

A. Sk first vertical bar, TKS across (*26 lps on hook*);

B. ch 1, [yo, pull through 2 lps on hook] across.

Row 16: Rep row 15.

Last row: Sk first vertical bar, *insert hook under front vertical bar of next st and under top horizontal bar of next closing ch at same time, yo, pull through and pull through lp on hook (*sl st made*), rep from * across to last st, work sl st as for TKS in last st. Fasten off.

RIBBING
Repeat as for First Mitt.

FINISHING
Repeat as for First Mitt. ∎

VALENCIA
Wrap

SKILL LEVEL

INTERMEDIATE

FINISHED SIZE
17 x 100 inches at widest points

MATERIALS
- Universal Yarn Classic Chunky bulky (chunky) weight yarn (3½ oz/131 yds/100g per hank):
  8 hanks #60705 cherry tomato
- Size L/11/8mm Tunisian crochet hook, minimum length of 14 inches, or size needed to obtain gauge
- Size I/9/5.5mm crochet hook

GAUGE
Size L hook: 8 TKS = 3 inches; 5 TKS rows = 3 inches

PATTERN NOTES
Wrap is made starting from center back and working toward tip. Stitches are then picked up on opposite side of starting chain and worked toward opposite tip.

See Introduction for information on "mirror image" for left-handed crocheters.

Last loop on hook is counted as first loop of next row unless otherwise stated.

This project uses Right-Leaning 6-stitch cables (RLC). See pages 7 and 8 for detailed instructions.

SPECIAL STITCHES
Left leaning decrease (left leaning dec): Insert hook as for TKS in 2 sts at the same time, yarn over, pull loop through.

Right leaning decrease (right leaning dec): Skip next stitch, using hook, pull next stitch toward stitch just skipped until it sits on top of skipping stitch and in position in which hook can now be inserted in both stitches at the same time, yarn over, pull loop through.

WRAP
FIRST SIDE
Row 1:

A. With size L hook, ch 50, work **typical foundation** *(see page 4) (50 lps on hook)*;

B. ch 1, [yo, pull through 2 lps on hook] across, **1 lp rem on hook** *(see Pattern Notes)*.

Row 2:

A. Sk first vertical bar, **TKS** *(see page 4)* across *(50 lps on hook)*;

B. ch 1, [yo, pull through 2 lps on hook] across.

Row 3: Rep row 2.

Row 4:

A. Sk first vertical bar, TKS across *(50 lps on hook)*;

B. ch 1, **RLC** *(see page 7)*, [yo, pull through 2 lps on hook] across to last 7 sts *(8 lps rem on hook)*, RLC, yo, pull through 2 lps.

Row 5: When creating all following rows, ignore the ch-1 sp in the center of each cable:

A. Sk first vertical bar, TKS across (*50 lps on hook*);

B. ch 1, [yo, pull through 2 lps on hook] 3 times, ch 1, [yo, pull through 2 lps on hook] across to last 4 sts (*5 lps rem on hook*), ch 1, [yo, pull through 2 lps on hook] 4 times.

Rows 6 & 7: Rep row 5.

Row 8:

A. Sk first vertical bar, 6 TKS, **left leaning dec** (*see Special Stitches*), TKS across (*49 lps on hook*);

B. ch 1, RLC, [yo, pull through 2 lps on hook] across to last 7 sts (*8 lps rem on hook*), RLC, yo, pull through 2 lps on hook.

Rows 9–11: Rep row 5.

Rows 12–143: [Rep rows 8–11 consecutively] 66 times, ending with 16 lps on hook.

Row 144: Rep row 8. (*15 lps on hook*)

Row 145:

A. Sk first vertical bar, 6 TKS, left leaning dec, 6 TKS (*14 lps on hook*);

B. ch 1, [yo, pull through 2 lps on hook] across.

Row 146:

A. Sk first vertical bar, 6 TKS, left leaning dec, 5 TKS (*13 lps on hook*);

B. ch 1, [yo, pull through 2 lps on hook] across.

Row 147:

A. Sk first vertical bar, 6 TKS, left leaning dec, 4 TKS (*12 lps on hook*);

B. ch 1, [yo, pull through 2 lps on hook] across.

Row 148:

A. Sk first vertical bar, 6 TKS, left leaning dec, 3 TKS (*11 lps on hook*);

B. ch 1, [yo, pull through 2 lps on hook] across.

Row 149:

A. Sk first vertical bar, 6 TKS, left leaning dec, 2 TKS *(10 lps on hook)*;

B. ch 1, [yo, pull through 2 lps on hook] across.

Row 150:

A. Sk first vertical bar, 6 TKS, left leaning dec, TKS *(9 lps on hook)*;

B. ch 1, [yo, pull through 2 lps on hook] across.

Row 151:

A. Sk first vertical bar, 4 left leaning dec *(5 lps on hook)*;

B. yo, pull through 5 lps on hook at same time. Fasten off.

2ND SIDE
Row 1:

A. Turn project to beg working in starting ch on opposite side of row 1, with size L hook, pick up lp in each ch as for TKS *(50 lps on hook)*;

B. ch 1, [yo, pull through 2 lps on hook] across.

Row 2:

A. Sk first vertical bar, TKS across *(50 lps on hook)*;

B. ch 1, [yo, pull through 2 lps on hook] across.

Row 3: Rep row 2.

Row 4:

A. Sk first vertical bar, TKS across *(50 lps on hook)*;

B. ch 1, RLC, [yo, pull through 2 lps on hook] across to last 7 sts *(8 lps rem on hook)*, RLC, yo, pull through 2 lps on hook.

Row 5: When creating all following rows, ignore the ch-1 sp in the center of each cable:

A. Sk first vertical bar, TKS across *(50 lps on hook)*;

B. ch 1, [yo, pull through 2 lps on hook] 3 times, ch 1, [yo, pull through 2 lps on hook] across to last 4 sts *(5 lps rem on hook)*, ch 1, [yo, pull through 2 lps on hook] 4 times.

Rows 6 & 7: Rep row 5.

Row 8:

A. Sk first vertical bar, TKS across to last 9 sts, **right leaning dec** *(see Special Stitches)*, 7 TKS *(49 lps on hook)*;

B. ch 1, RLC, [yo, pull through 2 lps on hook] across to last 7 sts *(8 lps rem on hook)*, RLC, yo, pull through 2 lps.

Rows 9–11: Rep row 5.

Rows 12–143: [Rep rows 8–11 consecutively] 66 times, ending with 16 lps on hook.

Row 144: Rep row 8 *(15 lps on hook)*.

Row 145:

A. Sk first vertical bar, 6 TKS, right leaning dec, 6 TKS *(14 lps on hook)*;

B. ch 1, [yo, pull through 2 lps on hook] across.

Row 146:

A. Sk first vertical bar, 5 TKS, right leaning dec, 6 TKS *(13 lps on hook)*;

B. ch 1, [yo, pull through 2 lps on hook] across.

Row 147:

A. Sk first vertical bar, 4 TKS, right leaning dec, 6 TKS *(12 lps on hook)*;

B. ch 1, [yo, pull through 2 lps on hook] across.

Row 148:

> **A.** Sk first vertical bar, 3 TKS, right leaning dec, 6 TKS *(11 lps on hook)*;
>
> **B.** ch 1, [yo, pull through 2 lps on hook] across.

Row 149:

> **A.** Sk first vertical bar, 2 TKS, right leaning dec, 6 TKS *(10 lps on hook)*;
>
> **B.** ch 1, [yo, pull through 2 lps on hook] across.

Row 150:

> **A.** Sk first vertical bar, TKS, right leaning dec, 6 TKS *(9 lps on hook)*;
>
> **B.** ch 1, [yo, pull through 2 lps on hook] across.

Row 151:

> **A.** Sk first vertical bar, 4 right leaning dec *(5 lps on hook)*;
>
> **B.** yo, pull through 5 lps on hook at same time. Fasten off.

FINISHING

If desired, completely immerse project in cool water, squeeze lightly, roll in clean towel to remove excess water, lay flat, shape and allow to air dry. ∎

SKILL LEVEL

FINISHED SIZE
13 x 63 inches

MATERIALS
- Red Heart Super Tweed medium (worsted) weight yarn (5 oz/207 yds/140g per skein):
  4 skeins #7803 blue bayou
- Size L/11/8mm Tunisian crochet hook, minimum length of 14 inches, or size needed to obtain gauge
- Size I/9/5.5mm crochet hook

4 MEDIUM

GAUGE
Size L hook: 15 pattern sts = 4 inches; 13 pattern rows = 4 inches

PATTERN NOTES
Wrap is made vertically from 1 short edge to other short edge.

See Introduction for information on "mirror image" for left-handed crocheters.

Last loop on hook is counted as first loop of next row unless otherwise stated.

This project uses both Right-Leaning 6-stitch cables (RLC) and Left-Leaning 6-stitch cables (LLC). See page 7 and 8 for detailed instructions.

SPECIAL STITCHES
Tunisian Cross Stitch (TCS): Sk next ch-1 sp, insert hook from front to back under next ch-1 sp, yo, pull lp through, insert hook from front to back under ch-1 sp just sk, yo, pull lp through (2 sts created).

LIMERICK Wrap

Tunisian Puff Stitch (Puff): Insert hook from front to back under ch-1 sp, yo, pull lp through, yo, insert hook from front to back under same ch-1 sp, yo, pull lp through (3 sts created).

WRAP

Row 1:

A. With size L hook, ch 50, work **typical foundation** (*see page 4*), (*50 lps on hook*);

B. ch 1, [yo, pull through 2 lps on hook] across, **1 lp rem on hook** (*see Pattern Notes*).

Row 2:

A. Sk first vertical bar, **TPS** (*see page 5*) across (*50 lps on hook*);

B. ch 1, [yo, pull through 2 lps on hook] across.

Rows 3 & 4: Rep row 2.

Row 5:

A. Sk first vertical bar, 2 **TTPS** (*see page 5*), 6 **TKS** (*see page 4*), 2 TTPS, 3 TKS, 2 TTPS, 18 TKS, 2 TTPS, 3 TKS, 2 TTPS, 6 TKS, 2 TTPS, TKS (*50 lps on hook*);

B. ch 1, [yo, pull through 2 lps on hook] across.

Row 6:

A. Sk first vertical bar, 2 TTPS, 6 TKS, 2 TTPS, 3 TKS, 2 TTPS, 18 TKS, 2 TTPS, 3 TKS, 2 TTPS, 6 TKS, 2 TTPS, TKS (*50 lps on hook*);

B. ch 1, [yo, pull through 2 lps on hook] 10 times, ch 1, yo, pull through 4 lps (*3 sts closed here and throughout*), ch 1, [yo, pull through 2 lps on hook] 22 times, ch 1, yo, pull through 4 lps on hook, ch 1, [yo, pull through 2 lps on hook] 11 times.

Row 7:

A. Sk first vertical bar, 2 TTPS, 6 TKS, 2 TTPS, **TCS** (*see Special Stitches*), 2 TTPS, 18 TKS, 2 TTPS, TCS, 3 TKS, 2 TTPS, 6 TKS, 2 TTPS, TKS (*48 lps on hook*);

B. ch 1, [yo, pull through 2 lps on hook] 11 times, ch 1, [yo, pull through 2 lps on hook] 24 times, ch 1, [yo, pull through 2 lps on hook] 12 times.

Row 8:

A. Sk first vertical bar, 2 TTPS, 6 TKS, 2 TTPS, **puff** (*see Special Stitches*), 2 TTPS, 18 TKS, 2 TTPS, puff, 2 TTPS, 6 TKS, 2 TTPS, TKS (*50 lps on hook*);

B. ch 1, [yo, pull through 2 lps on hook] twice, **RLC** (*see page 7*), [yo, pull through 2 lps on hook] 10 times, RLC, **LLC** (*see page 8*), [yo, pull through 2 lps on hook] 10 times, RLC, [yo, pull through 2 lps on hook] 3 times.

Row 9: When creating all following rows, ignore the ch-1 sp in the center of each cable:

A. Sk first vertical bar, 2 TTPS, 6 TKS, 2 TTPS, 3 TKS, 2 TTPS, 18 TKS, 2 TTPS, 3 TKS, 2 TTPS, 6 TKS, 2 TTPS, TKS (*50 lps on hook*);

B. ch 1, [yo, pull through 2 lps on hook] 5 times, ch 1, [yo, pull through 2 lps on hook] 16 times, ch 1, [yo, pull through 2 lps on hook] 6 times, ch 1, [yo, pull through 2 lps on hook] 16 times, ch 1, [yo, pull through 2 lps on hook] 6 times.

Row 10:

A. Sk first vertical bar, 2 TTPS, 6 TKS, 2 TTPS, 3 TKS, 2 TTPS, 18 TKS, 2 TTPS, 3 TKS, 2 TTPS, 6 TKS, 2 TTPS, TKS (*48 lps on hook*);

B. ch 1, [yo, pull through 2 lps on hook] 5 times, ch 1, [yo, pull through 2 lps on hook] 5 times, ch 1, yo, pull through 4 lps, ch 1, [yo, pull through 2 lps on hook] 8 times, ch 1, [yo, pull through 2 lps on hook] 6 times, ch 1, [yo, pull through 2 lps on hook] 8 times, ch 1, yo, pull through 4 lps on hook, ch 1, [yo, pull through 2 lps on hook] 5 times, ch 1, [yo, pull through 2 lps on hook] 6 times.

Row 11:

   A. Sk first vertical bar, 2 TTPS, 6 TKS, 2 TTPS, TCS, 2 TTPS, 18 TKS, 2 TTPS, TCS, 3 TKS, 2 TTPS, 6 TKS, 2 TTPS, TKS *(48 lps on hook)*;

   B. ch 1, [yo, pull through 2 lps on hook] 5 times, ch 1, [yo, pull through 2 lps on hook] 6 times, ch 1, [yo, pull through 2 lps on hook] 9 times, ch 1, [yo, pull through 2 lps on hook] 6 times, ch 1, [yo, pull through 2 lps on hook] 9 times, ch 1, [yo, pull through 2 lps on hook] 6 times, ch 1, [yo, pull through 2 lps on hook] 6 times.

Row 12:

   A. Sk first vertical bar, 2 TTPS, 6 TKS, 2 TTPS, puff, 2 TTPS, 18 TKS, 2 TTPS, puff, 2 TTPS, 6 TKS, 2 TTPS, TKS *(50 lps on hook)*;

   B. ch 1, [yo, pull through 2 lps on hook] twice, RLC, [yo, pull through 2 lps on hook] 10 times, LLC, RLC, [yo, pull through 2 lps on hook] 10 times, RLC, [yo, pull through 2 lps on hook] 3 times.

Row 13:

   A. Sk first vertical bar, 2 TTPS, 6 TKS, 2 TTPS, 3 TKS, 2 TTPS, 18 TKS, 2 TTPS, 3 TKS, 2 TTPS, 6 TKS, 2 TTPS, TKS *(50 lps on hook)*;

   B. ch 1, [yo, pull through 2 lps on hook] 5 times, ch 1, [yo, pull through 2 lps on hook] 13 times, ch 1, [yo, pull through 2 lps on hook] 12 times, ch 1, [yo, pull through 2 lps on hook] 13 times, ch 1, [yo, pull through 2 lps on hook] 6 times.

Row 14:

   A. Sk first vertical bar, 2 TTPS, 6 TKS, 2 TTPS, 3 TKS, 2 TTPS, 18 TKS, 2 TTPS, 3 TKS, 2 TTPS, 6 TKS, 2 TTPS, TKS *(50 lps on hook)*;

   B. ch 1, [yo, pull through 2 lps on hook] 5 times, ch 1, [yo, pull through 2 lps on hook] 5 times, ch 1, yo, pull through 4 lps on hook, ch 1, [yo, pull through 2 lps on hook] 5 times, ch 1, [yo, pull through 2 lps on hook] 12 times, ch 1, [yo, pull through 2 lps on hook] 5 times, ch 1, yo, pull through 4 lps on hook, ch 1, [yo, pull through 2 lps on hook] 5 times, ch 1, [yo, pull through 2 lps on hook] 6 times.

Row 15:

   A. Sk first vertical bar, 2 TTPS, 6 TKS, 2 TTPS, TCS, 2 TTPS, 18 TKS, 2 TTPS, TCS, 3 TKS, 2 TTPS, 6 TKS, 2 TTPS, TKS *(48 lps on hook)*;

   B. ch 1, [yo, pull through 2 lps on hook] 5 times, ch 1, [yo, pull through 2 lps on hook] 6 times, ch 1, [yo, pull through 2 lps on hook] 6 times, ch 1, [yo, pull through 2 lps on hook] 12 times, ch 1, [yo, pull through 2 lps on hook] 6 times, ch 1, [yo, pull through 2 lps on hook] 6 times.

Rows 16–199: [Rep rows 8–15 consecutively] 23 times.

Rows 200–204: Rep rows 8–12.

Row 205:

   A. Sk first vertical bar, 2 TTPS, 6 TKS, 2 TTPS, 3 TKS, 2 TTPS, 18 TKS, 2 TTPS, 3 TKS, 2 TTPS, 6 TKS, 2 TTPS, TKS *(50 lps on hook)*;

   B. ch 1, [yo, pull through 2 lps on hook] across.

Row 206:

   A. Sk first vertical bar, TPS across *(50 lps on hook)*;

   B. ch 1, [yo, pull through 2 lps across.

Row 207: Rep row 206.

Final row: Sk first vertical bar, insert hook in next st as for TPS, yo, pull lp through st and through lp on hook *(sl st made)*, sl st as for TPS across to last st, sl st as for TKS in last st. Fasten off. ■

Metric
Conversion
Charts

METRIC CONVERSIONS

yards	x	.9144	=	metres (m)
yards	x	91.44	=	centimetres (cm)
inches	x	2.54	=	centimetres (cm)
inches	x	25.40	=	millimetres (mm)
inches	x	.0254	=	metres (m)

centimetres	x	.3937	=	inches
metres	x	1.0936	=	yards

INCHES INTO MILLIMETRES & CENTIMETRES (Rounded off slightly)

inches	mm	cm	inches	cm	inches	cm	inches	cm
1/8	3	0.3	5	12.5	21	53.5	38	96.5
1/4	6	0.6	5 1/2	14	22	56	39	99
3/8	10	1	6	15	23	58.5	40	101.5
1/2	13	1.3	7	18	24	61	41	104
5/8	15	1.5	8	20.5	25	63.5	42	106.5
3/4	20	2	9	23	26	66	43	109
7/8	22	2.2	10	25.5	27	68.5	44	112
1	25	2.5	11	28	28	71	45	114.5
1 1/4	32	3.2	12	30.5	29	73.5	46	117
1 1/2	38	3.8	13	33	30	76	47	119.5
1 3/4	45	4.5	14	35.5	31	79	48	122
2	50	5	15	38	32	81.5	49	124.5
2 1/2	65	6.5	16	40.5	33	84	50	127
3	75	7.5	17	43	34	86.5		
3 1/2	90	9	18	46	35	89		
4	100	10	19	48.5	36	91.5		
4 1/2	115	11.5	20	51	37	94		

KNITTING NEEDLES CONVERSION CHART

Canada/U.S.	0	1	2	3	4	5	6	7	8	9	10	10½	11	13	15
Metric (mm)	2	2¼	2¾	3¼	3½	3¾	4	4½	5	5½	6	6½	8	9	10

CROCHET HOOKS CONVERSION CHART

Canada/U.S.	1/B	2/C	3/D	4/E	5/F	6/G	8/H	9/I	10/J	10½/K	N
Metric (mm)	2.25	2.75	3.25	3.5	3.75	4.25	5	5.5	6	6.5	9.0

STITCH GUIDE

FOR MORE COMPLETE INFORMATION,
VISIT **ANNIESCATALOG.COM/STITCHGUIDE**

STITCH ABBREVIATIONS

beg	begin/begins/beginning
bpdc	back post double crochet
bpsc	back post single crochet
bptr	back post treble crochet
CC	contrasting color
ch(s)	chain(s)
ch-	refers to chain or space previously made (i.e., ch-1 space)
ch sp(s)	chain space(s)
cl(s)	cluster(s)
cm	centimeter(s)
dc	double crochet (singular/plural)
dc dec	double crochet 2 or more stitches together, as indicated
dec	decrease/decreases/decreasing
dtr	double treble crochet
ext	extended
fpdc	front post double crochet
fpsc	front post single crochet
fptr	front post treble crochet
g	gram(s)
hdc	half double crochet
hdc dec	half double crochet 2 or more stitches together, as indicated
inc	increase/increases/increasing
lp(s)	loop(s)
MC	main color
mm	millimeter(s)
oz	ounce(s)
pc	popcorn(s)
rem	remain/remains/remaining
rep(s)	repeat(s)
rnd(s)	round(s)
RS	right side
sc	single crochet (singular/plural)
sc dec	single crochet 2 or more stitches together, as indicated
sk	skip/skipped/skipping
sl st(s)	slip stitch(es)
sp(s)	space(s)/spaced
st(s)	stitch(es)
tog	together
tr	treble crochet
trtr	triple treble
WS	wrong side
yd(s)	yard(s)
yo	yarn over

YARN CONVERSION

OUNCES TO GRAMS	GRAMS TO OUNCES
1 .... 28.4	25 .... ⅞
2 .... 56.7	40 .... 1⅔
3 .... 85.0	50 .... 1¾
4 .... 113.4	100 .... 3½

UNITED STATES		UNITED KINGDOM
sl st (slip stitch)	=	sc (single crochet)
sc (single crochet)	=	dc (double crochet)
hdc (half double crochet)	=	htr (half treble crochet)
dc (double crochet)	=	tr (treble crochet)
tr (treble crochet)	=	dtr (double treble crochet)
dtr (double treble crochet)	=	ttr (triple treble crochet)
skip	=	miss

Single crochet decrease (sc dec): (Insert hook, yo, draw lp through) in each of the sts indicated, yo, draw through all lps on hook.

Example of 2-sc dec

Half double crochet decrease (hdc dec): (Yo, insert hook, yo, draw lp through) in each of the sts indicated, yo, draw through all lps on hook.

Example of 2-hdc dec

Reverse single crochet (reverse sc): Ch 1, sk first st, working from left to right, insert hook in next st from front to back, draw up lp on hook, yo, and draw through both lps on hook.

Chain (ch): Yo, pull through lp on hook.

Single crochet (sc): Insert hook in st, yo, pull through st, yo, pull through both lps on hook.

Double crochet (dc): Yo, insert hook in st, yo, pull through st, [yo, pull through 2 lps] twice.

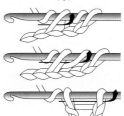

Double crochet decrease (dc dec): (Yo, insert hook, yo, draw lp through, yo, draw through 2 lps on hook) in each of the sts indicated, yo, draw through all lps on hook.

Example of 2-dc dec

Front loop (front lp) Back loop (back lp)

Front Loop   Back Loop

Front post stitch (fp): Back post stitch (bp): When working post st, insert hook from right to left around post of st on previous row.

Back   Front

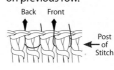

Post of Stitch

Half double crochet (hdc): Yo, insert hook in st, yo, pull through st, yo, pull through all 3 lps on hook.

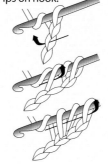

Double treble crochet (dtr): Yo 3 times, insert hook in st, yo, pull through st, [yo, pull through 2 lps] 4 times.

Treble crochet decrease (tr dec): Holding back last lp of each st, tr in each of the sts indicated, yo, pull through all lps on hook.

Example of 2-tr dec

Slip stitch (sl st): Insert hook in st, pull through both lps on hook.

Chain color change (ch color change) Yo with new color, draw through last lp on hook.

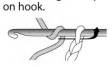

Double crochet color change (dc color change) Drop first color, yo with new color, draw through last 2 lps of st.

Treble crochet (tr): Yo twice, insert hook in st, yo, pull through st, [yo, pull through 2 lps] 3 times.

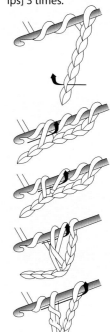

Annie's™ *Tunisian Cables to Crochet* is published by Annie's, 306 East Parr Road, Berne, IN 46711. Printed in USA. Copyright © 2012 Annie's. All rights reserved. This publication may not be reproduced in part or in whole without written permission from the publisher.

RETAIL STORES: If you would like to carry this publication or any other Annie's publications, visit AnniesWSL.com.

Every effort has been made to ensure that the instructions in this pattern book are complete and accurate. We cannot, however, take responsibility for human error, typographical mistakes or variations in individual work. Please visit AnniesCustomerCare.com to check for pattern updates.

ISBN: 978-1-59635-551-4

1 2 3 4 5 6 7 8 9